Building the Medieval Cathedrals

Percy Watson

Published in cooperation with Cambridge University Press
Lerner Publications Company, Minneapolis

Editors' Note: In preparing this edition of *The Cambridge Topic Books* for publication, the editors have made only a few minor changes in the original material. In some isolated cases, British spelling and usage were altered in order to avoid possible confusion for our readers. Whenever necessary, information was added to clarify references to people, places, and events in British history. An index was also provided in each volume.

LIBRARY OF CONGRESS CATALOGING IN PUBLICATION DATA

Watson, Percy.
Building the medieval cathedrals.

(A Cambridge Topic Book)
Includes index.
SUMMARY: Discusses the materials and methods used in building the great English cathedrals, the craftsmen who built them, and the styles in which they were built.

1. Cathedrals—England—Juvenile literature. 2. Architecture, Medieval—England—Juvenile literature. 3. Building—England—Juvenile literature. [1. Cathedrals—England. 2. Architecture, Medieval—England. 3. Building] 1. Title.

NA5463.W37 1979   726'.6'0942   78-56794
ISBN 0-8225-1213-0

This edition first published 1979 by Lerner Publications Company
by permission of Cambridge University Press.

Original edition copyright © 1976 by Cambridge University Press
as part of *The Cambridge Introduction to the History of Mankind: Topic Book*.

International Standard Book Number: 0-8225-1213-0
Library of Congress Catalog Card Number: 78-56794

Manufactured in the United States of America.

This edition is available exclusively from:
Lerner Publications Company, 241 First Avenue North, Minneapolis, Minnesota 55401

Contents

A bishop enthroned upon his chair, the cathedra that gives its name to the building.

1 Where they built and why

When William the Conqueror took over England in 1066, he planned to govern his new domain partly through the Catholic Church. In those days churchmen helped to run the country, so William took care to see that his bishops were efficient and trustworthy men. In 1070 Lanfranc was appointed Archbishop of Canterbury, head of the Church in England, and he reorganized the old Anglo-Saxon sees or dioceses (the areas controlled by bishops).

The cathedrals from which the bishops ruled their sees were generally in important trading centres since this was where most people lived. The word 'cathedral' comes from the Latin word *cathedra*, meaning a chair or throne, because it was from their chairs in these buildings that the early bishops taught Christianity.

The Normans found it necessary to move some of the Anglo-Saxon cathedrals to better positions and so well did they choose the new locations that few moves were required later in the Middle Ages. The various moves of the cathedral in what is now the see of Norwich illustrate the determination of Norman bishops to find the best possible centre for their work.

A similar move was made in the south of England where the cathedral was put in Old Sarum instead of Sherborne. Old Sarum was a fortified hill-top town of importance, but by 1228 the problems of working in a cramped military centre annoyed the bishop so much that the cathedral was moved down into the valley at Salisbury. You will read more about this change later.

English sees and their cathedrals in 1066

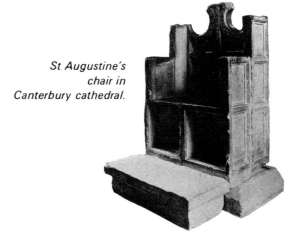

St Augustine's chair in Canterbury cathedral.

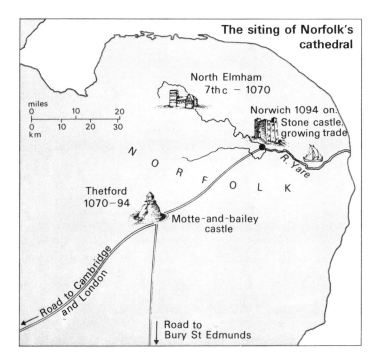

The siting of Norfolk's cathedral

North Elmham 7th c – 1070

Norwich 1094 on. Stone castle, growing trade

R. Yare

Thetford 1070–94

Motte-and-bailey castle

miles
0   10   20
0 10 20 30
km

N O R F O L K

Road to Cambridge and London

Road to Bury St Edmunds

above: *The foundations of the Norman cathedral at Old Sarum can still be seen, to the right of the castle mound, seven and a half centuries after they were abandoned.*

You can see from the map why the Normans twice moved Norfolk's cathedral to a new position.

left: *The air photograph shows how the cathedral was eventually built near the castle and the river that made Norwich an important town. The castle on its wooded hill is in the lower right-hand corner of this photograph, the cathedral to the left of centre.*

Durham cathedral as it may have looked in Norman times, strongly placed on its hill above the river.

Most cathedrals did not have to be moved because they had been well sited in earlier times. It would be difficult to imagine a better position for the government and defence of the warlike north than Durham. Before the cathedral was built at Durham other places had been tried. Viking raids had caused the monks to flee the island of Lindisfarne taking the body of St Cuthbert with them. Many years later their successors were in flight again and stopped at the place where Durham cathedral now stands. When the time came for them to move it is said that they found themselves unable to lift the saint's coffin and took this to be a sign that he had decided upon his final resting place; so they set about building a church. Certainly the rocky hill surrounded on three sides by the River Wear had excellent defensive possibilities and a general could not have chosen a better place!

Centres of activity

Cathedrals were the scene of many splendid state occasions: coronations, christenings, weddings, funerals and parliaments all took place within their walls. But it is the evidence of burials which remains for us today. Many powerful men were buried right in the cathedrals themselves. The ungodly William Rufus, son of the Conqueror, was buried at Winchester: the monks blamed the later collapse of their church tower on his presence. Often, people arranged for their bodies to be laid near the body of a favourite saint. King John, for example, is buried between St Oswald and St Wulfstan in the choir at Worcester. Probably the best known royal tomb is that of the Black Prince at Canterbury. It was beside that of St Thomas Becket, but Becket's tomb has been destroyed.

Because many cathedrals contained the bones of saints they were often visited by pilgrims seeking help or a cure for an illness. For some a pilgrimage was rather like a holiday but for others it was part of a punishment for a crime which they had committed. Many people in the Middle Ages tried to go on at least one pilgrimage since it was felt to be part of the duty of a good Christian. Cathedrals were planned to cope with the throngs of pilgrims who came there during the summer months. Probably the best known shrine in England was that of the murdered Becket. Another much-visited shrine was that of St Swithun, at Winchester. St William was a popular saint at Norwich; he was a young boy said to have been crucified by the local Jews. Other cathedrals had similar boy martyrs and it is difficult for us to know the truth about them. The Jews were often unpopular money lenders in those days and it is possible that the stories may have arisen out of attempts to discredit them, or more simply to divert attention from the real murderers.

The main work of the cathedral was to carry out a series of services every day. People in the Middle Ages believed that

Henry Chichele, archbishop of Canterbury from 1414 to 1443, had a great tomb built for himself in his cathedral. Why do you think he included these two very different effigies of himself?

right: *This thirteenth-century window at Canterbury shows pilgrims visiting the tomb of St Thomas; they can touch the saint's remains through the holes in the side of the tomb.*

only saints went straight to heaven and that ordinary folk were required to spend a period of time being punished in purgatory for the sins committed during their lifetime. Pilgrimages, offerings, crusades, attendance at special services and having masses said for one after death would, it was believed, help to shorten the time spent in purgatory. The men who offered up the cathedral services considered that they were helping the whole of mankind with their prayers. The great efforts made to make the cathedrals as magnificent as possible were not simply designed to impress people with the wealth and power of the Church; they were intended to show God how much men were prepared to do in His service.

The bishop gathered an army of axe-men.

Paying for the cathedrals

The money for building the great cathedrals came mainly from the rents on the lands which they owned, but there were many ways in which extra revenue could be obtained. Gifts were common: William the Conqueror himself gave the Bishop of Winchester permission to cut trees in the Royal Forest for four days. The wily bishop gathered a huge army of axe-men together and when the king found out how many trees had been felled he was horrified! The marble pillars round the Trinity Chapel, Canterbury, built soon after Thomas Becket was murdered, were a gift sent from Sicily by William the Good.

On a number of occasions the people of York subscribed vast sums of money for cathedral building. Bishop Peter d'Aquablanca of Hereford made himself very unpopular with his clergy by demanding a loan to help with rebuilding. King Henry II found that some of his nobles were too ready to leave property to the Church in their wills and so made laws to prohibit this without royal permission. When a cathedral suffered a disaster such as a fire or collapse messengers would be sent around the country to make appeals for money, and we can imagine that the tales which they could tell of godly men burned or crushed soon helped to swell the funds.

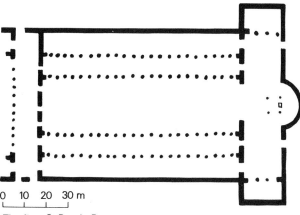

The first St Peter's, Rome
Built by Emperor Constantine, 4th century

0 10 20 30 m

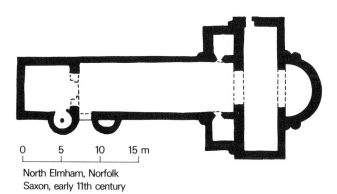

0   5   10   15 m

North Elmham, Norfolk
Saxon, early 11th century

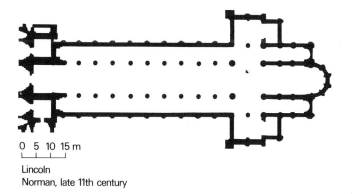

0 5 10 15 m

Lincoln
Norman, late 11th century

The Normans

In the years after the Normans arrived a great spate of new building work took place in England. Even where the cathedral remained on the Anglo-Saxon site, plans were made for a more splendid building. The Norman rulers were bursting with energy and new ideas in building. Perhaps it is not true to say that their ideas were new since another name given to the Norman style is 'Romanesque', meaning in a Roman style. Changes in building took place over many centuries and the Normans worked to a pattern which had started in Roman times and had been used in a rougher form during the several centuries of the Dark Ages. Nevertheless, the Normans were great builders and produced works on a scale which had not been known in Anglo-Saxon times. Their cathedrals were larger than any buildings since those of the last great Roman Emperors.

Ground plans of three great churches, one built by the Romans, one by Anglo-Saxons, one by Normans. The buildings differ very much in size, as you can see by comparing the scales, but they all follow the same general plan: a semi-circular apse around the altar at one end, and a long nave to hold the congregation, sometimes with aisles alongside it.

2 The Norman cathedral

Apse
Roof timbers
Stone vaulting
Transept chapel
Nave
Pillars
Aisle

In order to understand the way in which the medieval cathedral was built it is helpful to study a particular building, and Durham is a very good example of the Norman style. Even at Durham, however, there have been many changes since those times so that we must try to imagine the cathedral as it was at the end of the Norman period rather than as it is today.

The plan

The ground plan of Durham followed the usual pattern of the times. At the west front there were the two great towers common in France and much favoured by the Norman builders. Between the towers the west door led into the nave with its rows of stout pillars down each side and aisles behind them. Roughly half-way down the cathedral were the transepts to the north and south, and above the point where they crossed the nave was a third tower. Along the east walls of

The drawing with a section cut out shows Durham as it was built by the Normans between 1091 and 1133. The plan opposite shows the cathedral later in Norman times, with the Galilee Chapel added at the west end.

the transepts were a number of small chapels. Beyond the crossing was the choir, the east end of which ended in a semi-circle (apse) with the bishop's throne on a raised platform in the central archway behind the high altar.

In late Norman times it had been the intention to build a Lady Chapel (a chapel dedicated to Mary, the mother of Christ) beyond the apse but this had failed, probably as a result of poor foundations. The monks thought that the new work had collapsed because St Cuthbert, who mistrusted women and who was buried behind the high altar, was angry. Another chapel, known as the Galilee Chapel, was built at the west end instead. To the south of the cathedral church were the usual domestic buildings for the monks.

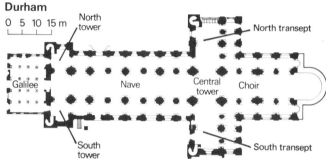

0 5 10 15 m

North tower

North transept

Galilee

Nave

Central tower

Choir

South tower

South transept

The nave of Durham, with massive early Norman pillars; and (right) the Galilee Chapel, with slender columns and richly decorated arches, added about seventy years later. When it was built each pillar had only two shafts; you can see how extra shafts, built up of lighter coloured stones, were added later to strengthen them.

11

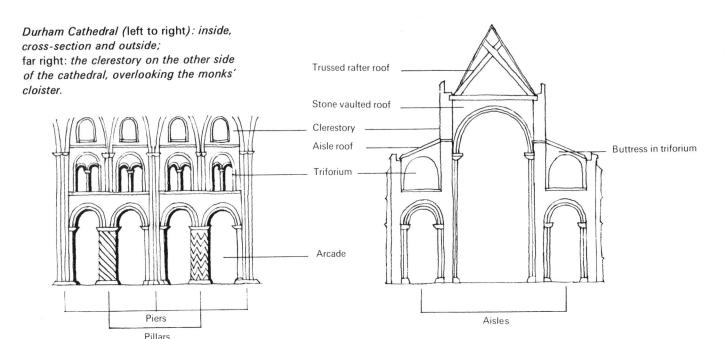

Durham Cathedral (left to right): inside, cross-section and outside; far right: the clerestory on the other side of the cathedral, overlooking the monks' cloister.

Trussed rafter roof

Stone vaulted roof

Clerestory

Aisle roof

Triforium

Arcade

Buttress in triforium

Piers

Pillars

Aisles

The nave was built in three levels: an arcade of pillars; a gallery known as the triforium in the middle; an upper row of windows called the clerestory (*clere* comes from the French word for light). The aisles beyond the pillars of the nave nearly doubled the floor space in the building. They did another very important job and that was to absorb the outward thrust caused by the weight of the roofing upon the main walls. The walls of the aisles were pierced by windows and near floor level was a low stone bench; people were expected either to stand or to kneel in the medieval churches but the old or infirm could 'go to the wall' in order to sit on this bench. The triforium was level with the roof of the aisles and because of this had no windows. Its arches added interest to the interior walls and the space behind them could be used as a gallery. The gallery was useful for maintenance work and for fire watching. A similar passage ran through the walls by the clerestory windows from which came most of the light for the nave.

Arches and towers

The interior roof of Durham cathedral was quite unusual in that it was finished in stone which hid the normal timber roof above. Most Norman buildings did not have this stone vault and it is thought that the masons at Durham were among the earliest to solve the problem of dealing with such a large span in this way. Stone vaults were usual for the aisles and quite common in small chapels. The invention was a very important one and its success depended upon the broad ribs of stone which supported the panels of lighter masonry and upon the use of pointed arches. The development was to lead to widespread use of the pointed arch and a whole new style of architecture.

Norman arches were semi-circular like the Roman ones from which they were copied. The semi-circular arch relies for its strength on the care with which the stones are chosen, cut and laid. It is important that the walls to either side of the arch are strong enough to withstand the powerful outward thrust which the weight of materials above the arch causes. Because of this Norman window arches were generally small in span and fairly widely spaced along the wall.

Building a central tower on a cathedral created special problems: from the outside a tower appears to be solid but it is really only supported at the corners. The lower sides of the tower are pierced by huge arches leading into the nave, the

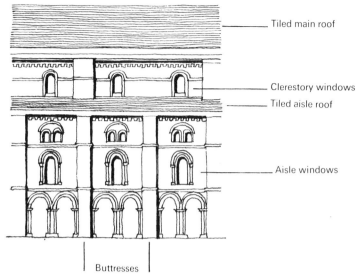

Tiled main roof

Clerestory windows

Tiled aisle roof

Aisle windows

Buttresses

choir and the two transepts. Large central towers were to become a very popular part of English cathedrals and this probably explains why the ground plan of an English cathedral is cross-shaped: the transepts act as buttresses to the nave and choir arches and so help them to carry the weight of the tower. The transepts gave extra room in the cathedral and it was usual for their eastern side to be divided into a number of small chapels. In Europe cathedrals tended to be made wider than in England and the two western towers, rather than a central one, continued to be important.

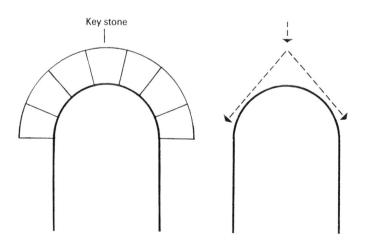

Key stone

How the weight of a stone wall, pierced by a round arch, is carried downwards *and* outwards. *The* buttress *helps to catch the dangerous outward thrust and to prop up the wall; but Norman buttresses were often badly planned, broad rather than deep.*

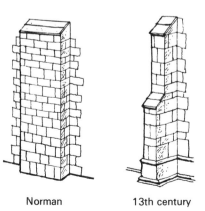

Norman   13th century

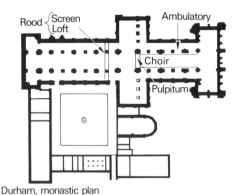

Durham, monastic plan

The plan of Durham Cathedral and its monastic buildings shows the rood screen *and the monks' door beyond it (see photograph) that led to the cloister, with the chapter-house, refectory and dormitory.*

Furnishings

It is difficult for us to imagine the furnishings of the Norman cathedral since no examples of this sort of Norman work remain. They were certainly of wood and because Durham cathedral was run by monks they would have followed the pattern usual for a monastic community. At the eastern end of the nave was a screen stretching from one wall to the other, on top of which would have been a huge cross ('rood') representing the crucifixion. This rood screen marked off the public from the monastic part of the cathedral. Pilgrims would have been allowed to pass through doors into the choir aisles (ambulatories) on special occasions in order to visit the shrine of St Cuthbert in the space behind the high altar. The rood screen also prevented the public from getting to the monks' private door into the cloister, which opened off the south aisle. In front of the rood screen would have been an altar which was used for public services in the nave.

Beyond the rood screen was another barrier about 15 feet (5 metres) high and stretching across the entrance to the choir. This was known as the 'pulpitum' (a Latin word meaning a raised platform) and it was several feet thick so that the top could be used as a gallery; it is thought that musicians would play there on important occasions. In the middle of the structure was a door leading into the choir which would be used for processions. It is probable that Norman pulpitums were simple wooden structures since none has survived.

Inside the choir were the stalls for the monks. The seats faced inwards, as do the choir stalls in the modern church, and each monk had his own place. The seats were probably quite simple stools since the elaborate fixtures which we can still see in some cathedrals were not developed till the thirteenth century.

In cathedrals run by canons (ordinary clergy) instead of monks the choir was generally smaller than at Durham and there was no rood screen, though there might be a beam level with the triforium stretching across to form a rood loft.

The interior of Norman Durham cathedral must have been quite dark because the windows were small, but even so, to the visitor of those days the effect of the red, black and gilt colour scheme, the bold pattern of repeated arches, the rich cloth hangings and the glass windows must have been breathtaking. Add to these experiences the extra light of a sunny day,

Few Norman furnishings remain, so these pictures show the more elaborate and substantial structures that replaced them. The pulpitum (above) was built in York Minster late in the fifteenth century in the Perpendicular style (see page 44). The wooden choir stall (right) at Worcester was made late in the Middle Ages; such stalls were made to tip up, and a ledge on the underside allowed the monk or canon, who had to stand for most of the service, to rest. This was called a misericord, meaning 'taking pity', and often the woodwork under the ledge was richly carved.

or the flickering of torches and the music of an evening service during an important festival, and we can appreciate how impressed the medieval visitor must have been with the power and the mystery of God and His church.

3 The workers and their task

The master mason

When a bishop decided to build he would appoint a master mason to take charge of the operation. At one time it was thought that the churchmen did the job themselves, but an examination of the building records of many cathedrals shows this idea to be mistaken. Masons guarded their trade secrets jealously and would not have welcomed too much interference; a French minstrel's song tells how a knight who tried to assist was beaten to death with masons' hammers!

The master mason was not only a skilled worker, he was also a good organizer: he had to arrange for supplies of stone, timber, lime, sand, lead and paint to arrive in time and in good condition; he had to control a labour force of masons, carpenters, carters, boatmen, tilers, plasterers and general labourers in such a way that they did the best possible work in the shortest time and at the most reasonable price.

The workers and guilds

News that a large cathedral was to be built soon spread and men would arrive seeking jobs, especially if the master mason had a high reputation. Sometimes the master mason would try to recruit men with whom he had worked in the past and whose work he knew he could rely upon. At times the king's need for masons to work on his castles resulted in a shortage of good labour since men were forced to join royal building works. If a bishop was a particularly powerful man he could sometimes persuade the king to allow his cathedral work to go on uninterrupted. Around the site a small township would develop because the workers knew that the building would take years to complete; they might even have work for a lifetime, so they brought their families with them.

In medieval times workers belonged to guilds and to some extent this helped the master mason since it meant that each

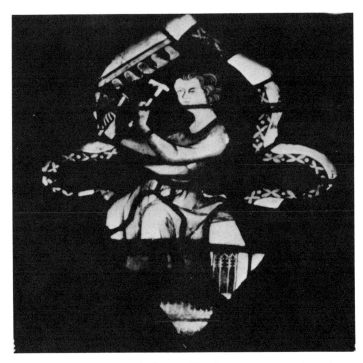

A fourteenth-century window at Ely shows a mason at work on stone tracery.

group of workers kept its own discipline and ensured that workmanship was sound, although the master mason still had to make sure that all of his different guildsmen worked as a team. Apprentices were required to take a number of tests before they became journeymen, that is, men hired by the 'day' (*jour* in French); and the guild tried to make sure that the men who trained apprentices kept to its standards. Apprentices and journeymen were bound to their masters by written agreements called 'indentures' which were cut apart after

hic collato memoria donatoris indelebi

Willegodum. Qu interpretat volens bonu

signing, along an 'indented' or wavy line, so that they could be matched up if there was any dispute. When workers first came to the job they took an oath before the master mason to work well and to follow the rules; this was often renewed by all the workers on 'pledgeday'.

A drawing from a thirteenth-century manuscript shows a king talking to his master mason, who carries square and dividers. Behind them workmen cut stone with axes, winch up stones in a basket, and check the level of the wall.

A modern artist has redrawn this scene for the front cover.

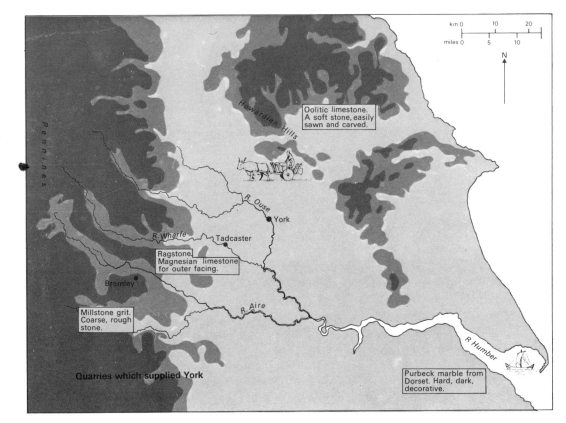

Oolitic limestone. A soft stone, easily sawn and carved.

Howardian Hills

Pennines

R. Ouse

York

R. Wharfe

Tadcaster

Ragstone. Magnesian limestone for outer facing.

Bramley

R. Aire

Millstone grit. Coarse, rough stone.

Quarries which supplied York

R. Humber

Purbeck marble from Dorset. Hard, dark, decorative.

The map shows the main places from which stone was brought for the building of York Minster. As far as possible it would be carried by barge or boat.

Materials

As the plans were agreed between the churchmen and their master mason, and as the first workers began to arrive, the problem of building materials became important. The size of the problem depended upon where the cathedral was sited, for not all areas had supplies of the right sort near at hand. In the Middle Ages great oak forests still covered much of England so that suitable timber could usually be found, but stone, lead and iron often had to be brought long distances. The cathedrals at Canterbury, Rochester and London (Old St Paul's) were built from stone brought from near Caen in France. The flints which were plentiful around Norwich were only suitable for rough work and all of the better stone was brought from the quarries at Barnack in Northamptonshire. Special stone such as Purbeck marble (really a dark limestone) came from near Corfe in Dorset and alabaster (a soft pale yellowish stone popular for making statues) came from Derbyshire. Lead and

Quarrying rough stone, from a painting in a fifteenth-century French manuscript.

copper also came from Derbyshire while iron was smelted in the Forest of Dean in Gloucestershire or the Weald of Kent and Sussex.

The mortar they needed was made from a mixture of sand, lime and water. Lime burners roasted chalk or limestone in large kilns in order to make quicklime. This was put into a large pit lined with clay, and water was added to it to turn it into slaked lime; from this the labourers made mortar.

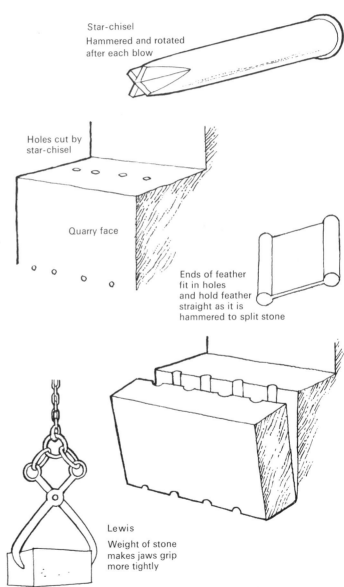

below: Some of the tools used by masons to cut and trim blocks of stone.

Star-chisel
Hammered and rotated
after each blow

Holes cut by
star-chisel

Quarry face

Ends of feather
fit in holes
and hold feather
straight as it is
hammered to split stone

Lewis
Weight of stone
makes jaws grip
more tightly

Marking out the foundations

As the first stone began to arrive the master mason would mark out the ground plan with the aid of wooden stakes, rope lines and a measuring pole. There is a popular legend that the east–west line of the church was decided by placing two stakes in line with the rising sun on the feast day of the particular saint to whom it was to be dedicated. Since the sun rises in a slightly different position in the east every day of the year this was thought to explain differences in line-up. Almost certainly this idea is false but if anybody did try let us hope that the sun shone on the morning when it was needed and that there were no hills or trees to the east to interrupt the view!

A series of squares marked out with the measuring pole and a rope triangle with sides 3, 4 and 5 units long would be used to determine right angles. Turf would be cut along the lines of the foundation trenches.

If the ground below the cathedral was rock, as at Durham and Lincoln, the builders were lucky. At Winchester the site was marshy and rafts of beech logs were laid in the mud; during the nineteenth century the wood rotted and had to be replaced with more modern foundations. Most buildings sank a little after they had been finished, but provided that they sank evenly all was well.

The masons

The masons began to build upwards as soon as the master mason was satisfied with the foundations. The making of the squared blocks of masonry (ashlar) was the responsibility of the freemasons, perhaps the most important workers on the site. There are two possible explanations of why they had this name: firstly, they worked in freestone; secondly, they were free to arrange their own terms of work. Freestone was so called because it could be worked fairly easily and it does not tend to split along natural lines as slate does. Generally free-

stone was either limestone or sandstone and varied in colour from nearly white or pale yellow to dark red.

The freemasons made the blocks and laid the more difficult stretches of wall while most of the building was done by the roughmasons. Only the outer and inner faces of the walls were built from shaped blocks, and the space between was filled with rough local stones and mortar. Because of this the walls were seldom as strong as they seemed since the core settled in a different way than did the outer stonework. In time the masons made tie-courses of squared ashlar which went right through the wall at intervals, giving added strength.

In early Norman times all masons used a tool rather like the modern fireman's axe for shaping stone but, though the roughmasons continued to use it, the freemasons changed to the use of a chisel and mallet for most jobs. The chisel had the advantage that it could be placed against the exact spot where material had to be removed and tapped very gently if necessary; special shapes of chisel could be used for different tasks. Gervase, the chronicler who reported on the rebuilding of Canterbury cathedral after the disastrous fire of 1174,

Wall construction

Rubble core, ashlar facing.

Early small square blocks, likely to crack above the joints. You can see how this happened in the Durham Galilee Chapel on p. 11.

Later, larger oblong blocks were used, trimmed to fit closely with thin layers of mortar.

A modern mason at work. Can you see the effect that the grooved edge of his chisel has on the surface of the stone?

Some of the mason's tools. Can you work out what each was used for?

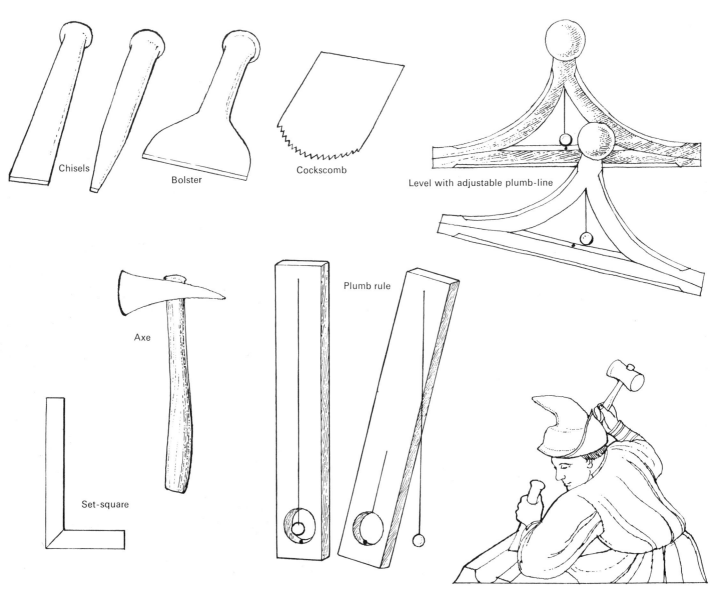

Chisels

Bolster

Cockscomb

Level with adjustable plumb-line

Axe

Plumb rule

Set-square

noted with enthusiasm the improved standard of workmanship produced with the chisel.

On wet days, and while the roughmasons were laying the walls, the freemasons worked at their heavy benches (bankers) in huts called lodges. So that the master mason could check their work it was usual for the freemasons to chisel their own banker mark on each block of stone. The highly skilled men who made the complicated pieces of stone used in window tracery and for arches do not seem to have been required to do this; perhaps this was because one man made the whole frame and his work could easily be recognised.

The plans for complicated jobs were made in the tracing house with the aid of large geometrical instruments. Often they were scratched on a plaster floor and then wooden or canvas patterns made for the freemasons to work from. As a window was completed the blocks would be laid out on the ground and when all of them were finished the mason would supervise their fitting together in position.

A roof boss, on the wooden ceiling of Winchester, shows a carpenter's hammer and pincers.

left: *A manuscript painting of the fifteenth century from Flanders shows scaffolding, a crane, a lewis, and the centring used in building an arch.*

As the walls rose scaffolding had to be erected and special frames (centring) made to support the arches while the mortar set. The masons knew that when the roof was put in place it would exert tremendous pressure outwards upon the walls. The arches and buttresses and parts of the building were made in such a way as to help withstand this pressure and to make the whole building as strong as possible. When a building had a vaulted stone roof extra care had to be taken because of the added weight. The medieval builders considered stone vaulting worthwhile because it reduced the risk of fire in the roof timbers and gave the inside a finished look.

Work on the high scaffolding could be dangerous because of the weight of the materials which the framework had to hold. William of Sens, the master mason responsible for the rebuilding work at Canterbury, fell from the scaffolding and was so badly injured that he was never able to work again.

The wrights

The wrights (carpenters) were the most important general craftsmen in medieval times. Although they were never the main workers on a cathedral site much of the job would have been impossible without them. Different sorts of wrights built houses, ships, bridges, quays, plows, carts, furniture and siege-engines. The masons building a cathedral relied upon the wrights for their scaffolding, hoists and centring, but the main job which the wrights had to do was the timberwork of the roof and the interior furnishings like the choir stalls, doors and screens.

Early in the building process the master wright arranged a store of specially selected beams and watched over them while they seasoned ready for the day, perhaps years later, when they would be used on the roof. Many of the beams were over 1 foot (300 mm) square and had been obtained by splitting the great oaks along their length with wedges. In those times

Carpenter's tools

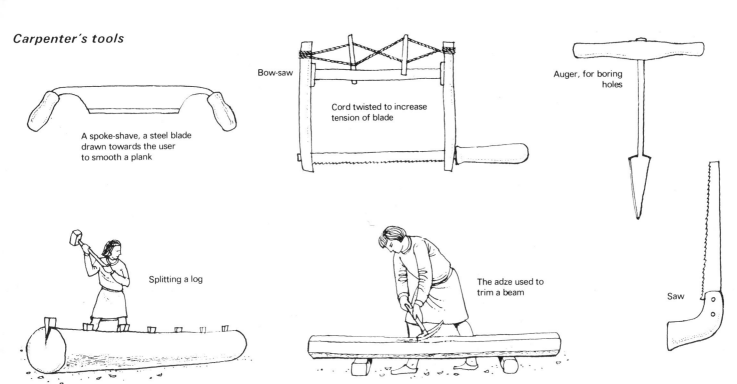

A spoke-shave, a steel blade drawn towards the user to smooth a plank

Bow-saw

Cord twisted to increase tension of blade

Auger, for boring holes

Splitting a log

The adze used to trim a beam

Saw

Saw-pit

sawing was a very slow and expensive job and, in any case, split timbers were stronger because they followed the grain. Once the trees had been split the beams were smoothed by the use of an adze. When planks were needed they were sawn from the roughly squared beams. The beam was placed over a pit so that one man could stand on top of it while his assistant worked the other end of the long two-handed saw. Naturally this was slow work. A common smoothing tool was the spoke-shave, a blade with a handle at each end which was pulled towards the worker.

The men who made the furnishings used tools very like the ones which would be used today, but you would probably have to go to a boatyard where wooden vessels are still made to see the tools used by the men who made the roof beams.

As the walls neared completion the wrights would start to prepare the joints on the roof rafters and trusses in much the same way as the masons prepared the window tracery. All of the beams would be marked so that they could easily be fitted

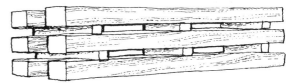

Beams were stacked and kept separate to dry and season

Roof beams at Salisbury. The doors at the end give some idea of the size of these timbers. Some are original beams, split and trimmed with an adze; others are modern saw-cut replacements. Can you see the difference?

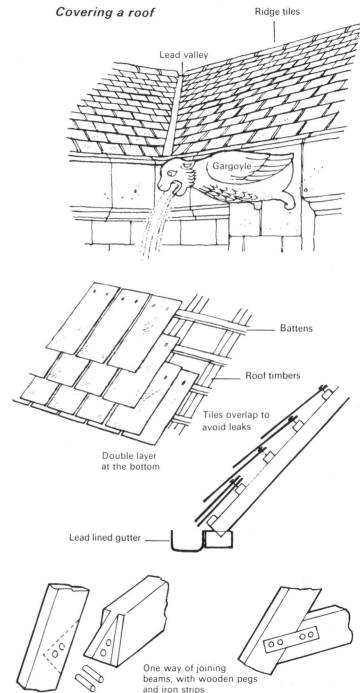

Covering a roof

Ridge tiles

Lead valley

Gargoyle

Battens

Roof timbers

Tiles overlap to avoid leaks

Double layer at the bottom

Lead lined gutter

One way of joining beams, with wooden pegs and iron strips

together once they had been hoisted to the roof. When they were in position the joints were secured with wedges and stout wooden pegs with, perhaps, iron straps made by the blacksmiths to give added strength.

Tiles, slates or lead were used for permanent roof coverings. So that the water would run off tile and slate roofs without seeping through, the roofs were quite steeply sloped, but as lead came into use more widely in the later Middle Ages roofs became less steep in pitch. Even on tiled roofs it was usual for the gutters and valleys to be finished in lead sheeting. The gutters led to gargoyles, stone spouts shaped into weird monsters, designed to shoot the rainwater clear of the walls, for downspouts were uncommon. If money was in short supply, or if a temporary covering was needed for the roof it might be thatched or covered with shingles. Shingles were wooden tiles and had been a common roofing material in Anglo-Saxon times.

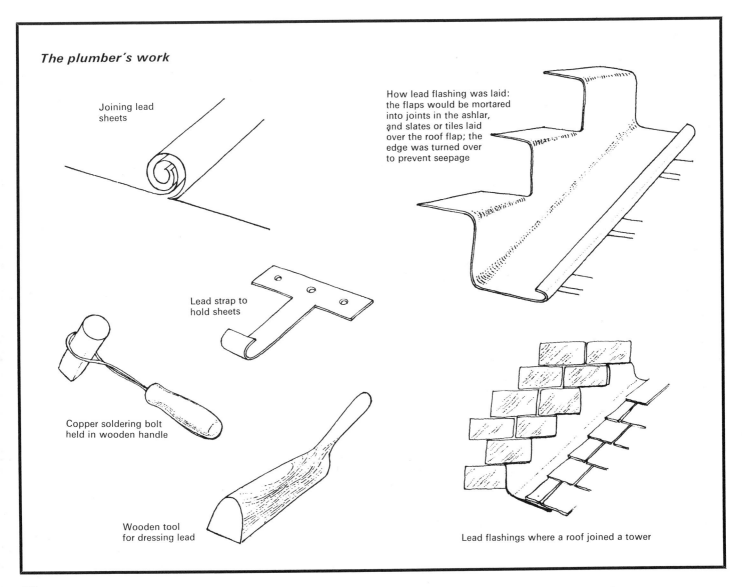

The plumber's work

Joining lead sheets

How lead flashing was laid: the flaps would be mortared into joints in the ashlar, and slates or tiles laid over the roof flap; the edge was turned over to prevent seepage

Lead strap to hold sheets

Copper soldering bolt held in wooden handle

Wooden tool for dressing lead

Lead flashings where a roof joined a tower

The plumbers

The work of the plumbers, or metal workers, (the name comes from the Latin word for lead, *plumbum*) was particularly skilful, especially when they had to cover with lead one of the huge wooden spires put up by the wrights. Unfortunately, these have all disappeared, although the one on Old St Paul's in London, which collapsed in the Great Fire during the sixteenth century, was 450 feet (150 metres) tall. A twelfth-century sketch of Canterbury Cathedral shows a tall wooden spire topped with a high gilded angel which could be seen for miles around. The lead-clad spires must have attracted lightning and it is not surprising that they have all gone; the tales of molten lead showering down during fires make exciting reading.

The plumbers prepared their own sheet lead from 'pigs' (cast slabs rather like long loaves). Once the lead had been made molten over a charcoal brazier it would be carefully and evenly poured on to a level bed of specially prepared sand. The sheet of lead would be made about 3 feet (1 metre) wide, several feet long and about ⅛ inch (4 mm) thick. The sheets were laid lengthwise up the roof starting from the bottom. The sheets were nailed to the roof, each sheet overlapping the top edge of the sheet further down. Sometimes, instead of overlapping the sheets, they would make them into one long strip by a process known as lead burning; a soldering iron would be used to weld the sheets together. The sheets were joined to those on either side of them by simply rolling the two edges together so that a tube about 2 inches (50 mm) in diameter appeared to run from top to bottom of the roof. The lead sheeting for valleys and gutters was cut to shape with shears and then tapped into position with wooden dressing mallets; in the gutters considerable skill at lead burning was needed.

It might be imagined that a lead-covered roof would last almost for ever, but unhappily this is not the case. There are two main reasons for failure: the tannin in oak timbers attacks the lead; and changes in temperature cause the lead to expand and contract so that in time cracks appear. Under a hot sun the lead expands and spreads down the roof, and when it cools in the evening it never returns exactly to its original position. The process is known as 'creep' and though it works very slowly it eventually spoils the lead so that it has to be re-cast. The shallower-pitched roofs of the later Middle Ages helped to reduce the effect of creep. Overlapping allowed creep to take place without causing as much damage as it would have done with long lead-burned strips. Also, hooks of lead called straps were used to support the lower edges of the sheets. Still, after about 150 years lead roofs had to be stripped, the lead melted down, and new lead added to replace that which had corroded away; then the lead had to be re-cast into new sheets and finally relaid.

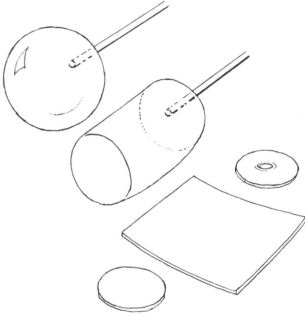

A fifteenth-century drawing shows the processes of glass-making.

Glass blowing: glass is blown on the pipe into a bubble or a cylinder, then cut and unrolled.

The glaziers

The earliest cathedrals had quite small windows and it was usual to have wooden shutters as an extra protection in bad weather. Glass was very expensive and often sheets of oilskin (linen painted with linseed oil) were used instead. The oilskins were yellowish in colour and in order to prevent them from flapping in a wind they were tacked to criss-crossed laths of wood. The earliest glass windows (grisaille) were often

arranged into a similar pattern and the colours were limited to pale yellow, greys and greens.

In the Middle Ages large sheets of glass could not be made. A glass blower would pick up a blob of molten glass on his blowing pipe and blow it into a large bubble. While the glass was still hot he would shape it into either a disc or a cylinder which was cut and flattened into small panes which were then allowed to cool. The earliest colours in grisaille were often the result of accidental impurities in the sand from which the glass

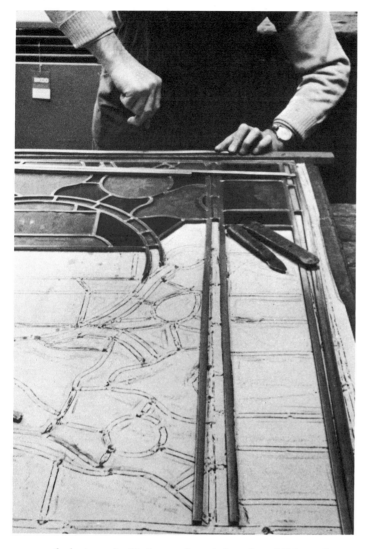

A modern glazier fitting together a window.

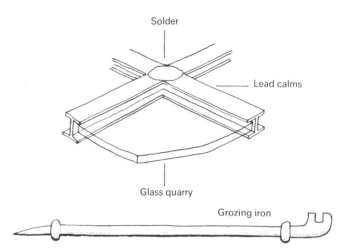

was made but gradually it was found that the addition of certain chemicals to the melting pot resulted in vivid colours.

The glaziers who designed the windows would sketch out their plan on a bench and then select small pieces of glass (quarries) in colours which pleased them to make up the pattern. Where quarries needed shaping to fit each other, a grozing iron was used. A grozing iron was rather like an iron pencil with a small wrench at one end. It was used by heating the pointed end and then passing it slowly across the quarries where a crack was needed; the crack would be made by cooling the heated part of the glass with water. This was a very slow process, and often the wrench-shaped end of the grozing iron was needed to snap off small pieces of the glass. Later it was found that glass cracked more easily if it was scratched with a diamond along the line where the break was intended.

When the glaziers wanted to put details on the glass they made a special paint out of gum-arabic, powdered glass and the colouring chemical. The details would be painted on and allowed to dry. The quarries would then be placed in a small furnace and heated till the gum-arabic burned off and the rest of the mixture fused into the glass; care had to be taken to ensure that the quarries were not over-heated or they would melt.

The pieces of the window were assembled on the bench and joined together with strips of lead called calms. Though much of this work could be done on the bench the job had to be finished in position and made waterproof with putty. The masons fitted iron or bronze bars across the stonework of the windows at intervals and the calms were wired to these as an added protection against strong gusts of wind.

The great west window at York Minster, more than 50 feet (16 metres) high, was completed in 1338 and filled with richly coloured glass. The two glass panels come from Canterbury Cathedral, and were made early in the thirteenth century. They are part of a 'Poor Man's Bible', telling the story of the New Testament for those who could not read it. Can you recognize the stories told here? You will find them in St Matthew's Gospel, chapters 2 and 13.

The tomb effigy of William of Wykeham, a great Bishop of Winchester who died in 1404, is painted in the brilliant colours of the vestments he wore in life.

The bishop painted on the wall of the Galilee Chapel at Durham in the twelfth century is supposed to represent St Cuthbert.

Decorating the walls

The walls inside cathedrals were usually plastered so that the smooth finish could be painted. Even woodwork was plastered with a thin layer of a special plaster known as gesso so that the grain and adze marks were smoothed out. In many cathedrals a change in fashion has resulted in the plaster being removed so that the medieval paintings have vanished. Perhaps the best way for us to understand what a medieval cathedral must have been like soon after it was built is to look at some of the illustrations in the manuscripts of the times. A few murals (wall paintings) remain, and with a little imagination they can give us an idea of how the buildings were decorated. It is surprising how many scraps of paint can still be found in corners, cracks in timber and between carvings on tombs in cathedrals today. The paintings of a bishop, said to be St Cuthbert, in Durham, and of St Paul in Canterbury are perhaps the best examples of early murals remaining.

The medieval painter ground his own colours and mixed his own paint. The large amount of money which was allocated to painting materials in the cathedral accounts tells us that a great deal of this work must have been done and that it was regarded as very important. For grinding the pigments the painters used small mill stones and mortars and pestles. Their brushes were very like ours today; the bristles were of hog's hair, badger's bristle or squirrel's hair.

There were different kinds of painters. The rough work was done by daubers and they also prepared the walls for the mural painters. Much gold leaf was used; gold can be hammered out into leaves thinner than paper which can then be stuck to things so that they appear to be made out of pure gold. Many medieval paintings had large areas of gold leaf and very impressive they must have looked.

The pictures on pages 34–6 show the work of some of the skilled craftsmen who helped to furnish the cathedrals.

The richly decorated font at Hereford was carved in Norman times. The base on which it stands is Victorian. The bishop's chair, also in Hereford, is said to date from Norman times or very soon after. One of the few pieces of Norman furniture to survive, all its spindles were made on a lathe.

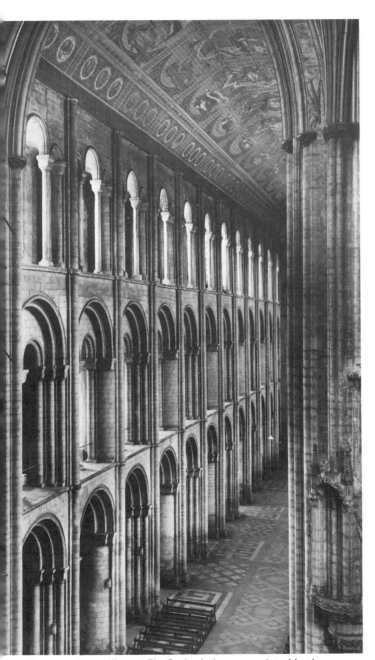

The wooden ceiling at Ely Cathedral was repainted in the nineteenth century, but many medieval cathedrals were painted like this.

These painted panels (or retable*) from behind an altar at Norwich were set up about 1381, with scenes from the Crucifixion and Resurrection.*

Other craftsmen

Many other craftsmen were needed to complete a cathedral but we can only mention them briefly.

Rich cloth hangings were common furnishings and they were frequently embroidered with gold thread and semi-precious stones. Sometimes they would be gifts from nunneries, for English nuns were famous for the quality of their threadwork. The vestments in which the body of St Cuthbert was clothed, preserved in the museum at Durham Cathedral, are good examples of this work and it is thought that even the famous Bayeux Tapestry was the work of English nuns.

Brass founders made altar furnishings, screens and lecterns. Jewellers, silversmiths, goldsmiths and enamellers combined to enrich shrines and produce sacred vessels. Enamellers decorated metal articles with brightly coloured glass.

Bell founders cast and hung huge bells; at Exeter the bells weigh $15\frac{1}{2}$ tons. Most cathedrals had organs. We know very little about early medieval organs except that most of them could be carried and therefore must have been quite small. Winchester, however, had an organ which had four hundred pipes and it is said that it required three organists and seventy blowers to play.

Locksmiths made intricate locks for doors and treasuries. In a few cathedrals, Exeter and Durham for example, there were large and complicated locks.

For every skilled man on the site there might be several labourers and it was their job to do all the pushing and pulling, fetching and carrying for the craftsmen. Today many of the jobs which they did would be done by machinery but in the Middle Ages labour was cheap and no doubt the local people welcomed the opportunity for jobs which a large building project provided.

The bronze effigy of the Black Prince at Canterbury was made by skilled craftsmen in the fourteenth century.

The iron lock-plate on the door of a fifteenth-century chapel at Winchester.

The clock inside Wells Cathedral was made about 1390. It has a 24-hour dial, and each time it strikes the armed horsemen above ride round through the arched openings, one knocking the other down. The 'sun' in the outer circle points to the hour, a star in the next circle shows the minute, and the innermost circle shows the day of the month.

Repairs and weaknesses

From the day that a cathedral was built the danger of collapse and fire was a constant worry to the clergy. Lightning or the careless use of candles and torches might cause a fire to start at any time, and once the fire had got a good hold on dry beams there was little that men could do with the primitive fire-fighting equipment of those times.

The great round Norman pillars look very strong but they suffered from the same weaknesses as the walls; only the outer masonry was shaped and the inside was a mixture of rubble and often inferior quality mortar. Faults in walls and pillars did not usually show at once but in time poor mortar changed back into sand. The fourteenth century was a particularly unhappy time for the monks of Ely: the early Norman central tower collapsed causing serious damage to the choir, and the late Norman north-west tower also fell. In many cases disasters were the result of adding height to towers which had not been designed to take the several thousand tons of extra masonry. In 1239 the canons of Lincoln were on very bad terms with their bishop. There is a story that one of them was preaching a sermon and had reached the point where, having already said some most unpleasant things about Bishop Grosseteste, he added, 'Were we silent the very stones would cry out for us'. The cathedral tower promptly crashed down killing three monks and seriously injuring several others. There must have been many near accidents which were prevented by the slow opening of cracks giving warning of danger before disaster struck. An evensong prayer ended with the words, 'deare Lord support our roof this night, that it may in no wise fall upon us and styfle us, Amen'.

At York Minster in the 1960s repairs costing two million pounds (almost four million dollars) became necessary as a result of weak foundations; the central tower, estimated to weigh 16,000 tons, is thought to have sunk 8 inches (200 mm) over the centuries while the rest of the building has only settled 4 inches (100 mm).

Wall paintings needed brightening with new paint from time to time and perhaps the plaster behind them might crack or be stained by damp. Water could seep in where lead had cracked or slipped or where tiles had been blown off in a gale, and before the damage had been noticed timber might start to rot or the mortar between the stones be spoiled. In the southern part of England the death-watch beetle could cause untold damage to timbers, and the only thing which could be done in those days was to replace the affected wood.

In order to prevent unnecessary damage and to simplify the work needed as a result of normal wear the builders made inspection passages along the clerestories, through the triforium and into the space between the stone roof vault and the roof timbers. In the thickness of the walls spiral staircases were provided to aid in inspection, repair and fire-fighting. At times of high fire risk, such as thunder storms and long dry spells, watchers would keep guard all night to make sure that if a fire did start it could be put out before it took firm hold. Cathedrals kept a permanent staff of workmen whose job it was to carry out inspections and do regular maintenance work. The keeping of such a staff was not without its problems; records show that the disorderly behaviour of the workmen sometimes worried the quiet monks of Norwich!

4 The Gothic cathedrals

Early English Gothic

The urge to build larger, stronger and more beautiful buildings was matched by the growing skill of the masons, a greater knowledge of geometry and the coming of new ideas from abroad. By 1200 a new style which we call 'Gothic' was replacing the Norman type of building. The name is rather misleading; it came into use while people admired the architecture of Greece and Rome and, since the Goths had been one of the warlike tribes who overthrew the Roman Empire, the word 'Gothic' suggested a barbaric departure from the civilized Roman work. We know this to have been a mistaken idea. As we shall see, Gothic architecture was a great advance in the Middle Ages.

Compared with Norman building the main features of the Gothic were: pointed arches, larger windows, thinner but stronger walls, the skilled use of buttresses and stone vaulted roofs. The advances in the new style came in gradually. The Cistercian order of monks, controlled from France, used pointed arches in many abbeys erected before 1200 though their buildings still had the heavy walls and wooden roofs characteristic of the Norman style. Contact with the Muslims in the Mediterranean, especially during the Crusades, must have taught European builders much; as early as 1130 a Muslim master mason, Lalys, was in charge of the work at Neath Abbey in South Wales. A number of books on geometry were translated from the Greek and Arabic at about this time.

The new cathedral built at Salisbury after the move from Old Sarum in 1220 was made in the style which we now call Early English Gothic and it is interesting to compare it with Norman Durham (*see* page 11). The basic plan is the same: the nave with its arcade on pillars, a triforium and a clerestory; transepts between the nave and choir; a stone vaulted roof. Yet the whole effect is quite different.

The use of the pointed arch resulted in a great increase in

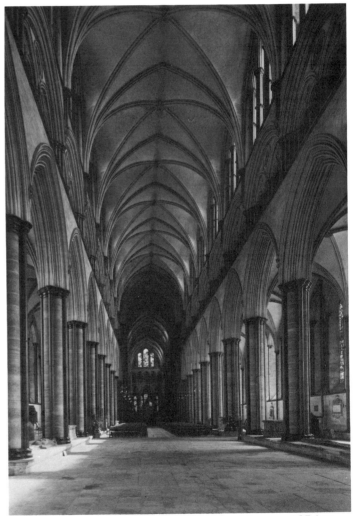

Salisbury's nave is over 200 feet (62 metres) long and 85 feet (27 metres) high. This photograph shows the choir stretching for another 200 feet beyond it.

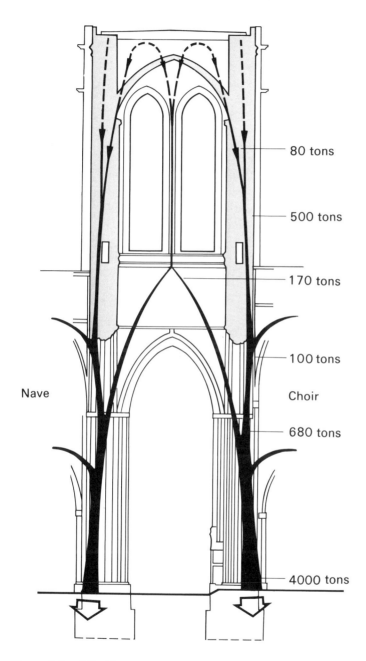

80 tons

500 tons

170 tons

Nave

100 tons

Choir

680 tons

4000 tons

The weight of York's great central tower is carried downwards by the pointed arches. Compare this with the diagrams of round arches on page 13.

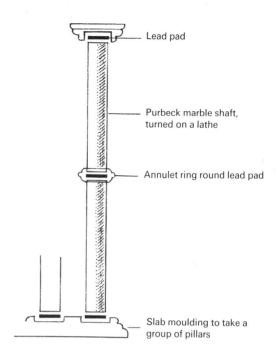

Lead pad

Purbeck marble shaft, turned on a lathe

Annulet ring round lead pad

Slab moulding to take a group of pillars

Salisbury's jointed shafting, described below.

strength because the thrust from the weight above was led downwards rather than outwards, and because of this the walls could be thinner than before. Where thrusts were strongest buttresses were used to absorb them, and at the corners stone pinnacles were added to give weight to withstand the strain.

A very popular feature of Early English Gothic which can be seen in Salisbury Cathedral is the use of Purbeck marble shafting. The dark polished stone makes an attractive contrast with the main masonry, adds strength and gives an impression of extra height. The shafts were put in position a few years after the main building was built so that it had time to settle. They were laid on discs of lead which formed a soft pad and prevented the ends of the shafts from shattering. Where shafts were jointed, 'annulet rings' of brass were used to prevent the lead discs from being squeezed out. The long shafts supporting Salisbury's central tower have actually been bent by the outward thrusts of the arches and tower above.

Salisbury

0 10 20m

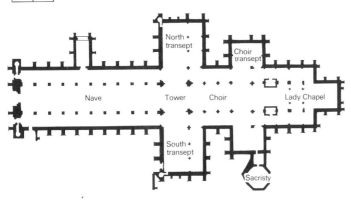

North transept

Choir transept

Nave   Tower   Choir   Lady Chapel

South transept

Sacristy

The plan of the east end of Salisbury represents a significant change from the Norman ground plan; this design is found only in English cathedrals. The idea may have come from the Cistercians and it had a number of advantages over the apse: it was easier to build, and easier to finish with a stone vault; a chapel could more easily be added to the east end and it allowed a large space (sometimes called a retro-choir) to be developed behind the high altar for the main shrine of the cathedral.

Many cathedrals had portions added to them in the Early English style. At Durham the Norman apse was removed and replaced by a broad chapel with nine altars by the same Bishop Poore who was responsible for the new cathedral at Salisbury. Rochester Cathedral was given new transepts and a crypt was made beneath the choir. Crypts are thought to have been inspired by the use of the catacombs (caves) around Rome during the days when Christians were persecuted. Generally they contained chapels but in the later Middle Ages a number of them were used to store bones which had been removed from the graveyard.

The crypt of Rochester.

A detail of the angel choir at Lincoln.

Decorated Gothic

For nearly a hundred years the sharply pointed Early English style was popular but the growing confidence of the masons and their increased skill in geometry led naturally to the kind of Gothic architecture which we call Geometrical Decorated. It is not really possible to illustrate this style so well with a single cathedral, although the choir at Lincoln is quite a good example.

In 1256, upon instructions from the Pope, work was started to provide the body of St Hugh of Lincoln with a more worthy resting place. The choir which St Hugh had built was demolished and a square-ended extension in the latest fashion was added. The new work became known as the Angel Choir because of the angels carved beside the triforium arches. It is easy to imagine the masons working with their compasses in the tracing house to produce the patterns for the arches and window tracery.

In later Decorated buildings the patterns did not follow such simple and regular lines and because of the new effect we call this Flowing or Curvilinear Decorated. The nave at York Minster, built about fifty years after Lincoln's Angel Choir, is in the later style. The west window, the west wall and the lower parts of the aisle are richly decorated in the new way (see the picture on page 32).

The triforium level, so important in Norman and earlier Gothic structures, was much reduced in size at York so that the effect is of two tiers rather than three. This was made possible because of the use of flying buttresses and lead aisle roof coverings. The flying buttresses caught the thrusts from the roof and carried them down to the ground almost as if a huge prop had been placed against the side of the building. Because the aisle roofs were finished in lead they did not need to have such a steep slope as for tiles and so the aisle and clerestory windows could be made larger. Nor was it neces-

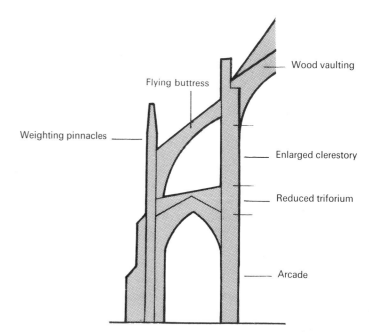

Wood vaulting

Flying buttress

Weighting pinnacles

Enlarged clerestory

Reduced triforium

Arcade

The flying buttresses of York.

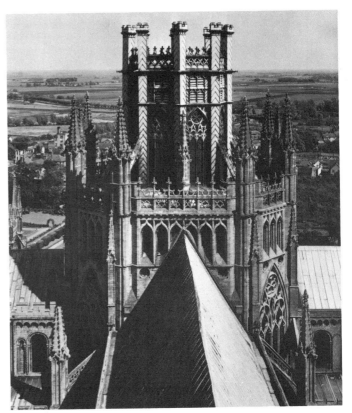

The richly decorated choir stalls of Winchester.

sary with flying buttresses to include reinforcing bridges in the triforium space.

The inner roof at York is particularly interesting since, though it is made of wood, it is designed to look like stone. We are not certain why the builders decided to finish the cathedral like this but it is thought that the original intention was to use stone. Perhaps the masons lost their nerve when faced with the 52-foot (17-metre) span, or perhaps the man who had to arrange payment for the work lost his nerve – we cannot say.

Some of the most magnificent Decorated work was done in wood and it often seems to copy the work of the masons in appearance. The choir stalls at Winchester look just like geometrical masonry, even down to the annulet rings!

Perpendicular Gothic

While the masons in the rest of Europe continued to experiment with a form of Decorated known as Flamboyant (flame like) the English masons launched themselves into the last development of the Gothic style. This last English style left: *The famous central Octagon Tower at Ely is unique and contains over 400 tons of wood and lead. Its construction was supervised by William Hurley, a master carpenter who had worked for Henry III. Originally the fine decorated stalls in the Ely choir stood below the well-lit space beneath the octagon.*

right: *The two photographs show the Norman arches at Winchester, which still remain in the transepts; and the arches in the new Perpendicular style that replaced them in the nave late in the fourteenth century.*
below: *You can see a drawing comparing the two styles.*

is known as Perpendicular or Rectilinear because of the fondness for lines running straight up and down and the frequent use of rectangular panels on walls, on roofs and in windows. It is almost as if the masons were trying to copy the methods of the wrights.

Winchester Cathedral shows the new development well because when repairs were needed to the crumbling Norman nave during the fourteenth century it was decided to use as much of the old stonework as possible in order to save money. Some of the Norman piers were chiselled into the Perpendicular pattern while others were stripped and recased in new stone. The round-headed arches of the Norman arcade were replaced by taller perpendicular arches so that the triforium practically disappeared and the clerestory windows were much enlarged. Because the pillars were reshaped rather than rebuilt they are rather thicker than normal Perpendicular work, but it would be difficult for the visitor today to guess what had happened.

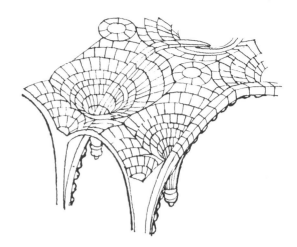

Fan vaulting seen from above.

The introduction of a new style of roof vaulting was, perhaps, the most spectacular invention of the Perpendicular masons. The earlier many-ribbed vaulting did not match the rectangles of the Perpendicular style and fan vaulting represented an attempt to make the patterns match throughout the whole building. In fan vaulting every single stone had to be a snug fit with its neighbours whereas in the earlier styles this was less important provided that the ribs were soundly made; the ribs in fan vaulting are chiefly for decoration.

Most cathedrals contain some features, often chantry chapels, in the Perpendicular style. Chantry chapels were common in the later Middle Ages and at their altars priests offered a daily round of prayers for the soul of a dead person. At Durham the chantry of Bishop Hatfield is combined with the bishop's throne and is of particular interest because it is painted in bright colours. The pulpitum in York (*see* page 15) was built right at the end of the fifteenth century in the Perpendicular style. The richly carved statues are portraits of English kings and all except one of the statues are original.

So skilled were the Perpendicular masons that they were able to reduce wall areas to a minimum so that windows almost replaced them. Thrusts were carried to the ground by cunningly placed buttresses and flying buttresses so that the

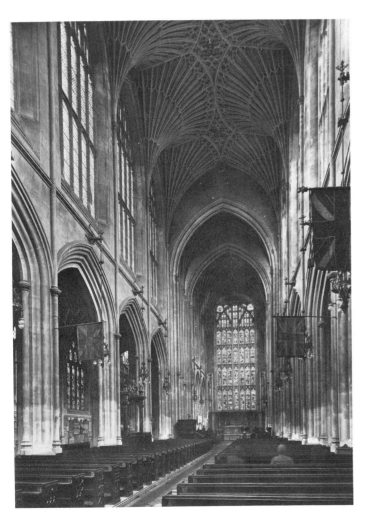

The choir of Bath Abbey, which was begun early in the sixteenth century, shows how well the fan vaulting matched the decoration on the walls and in the windows. The east wall seems to consist almost entirely of glass.

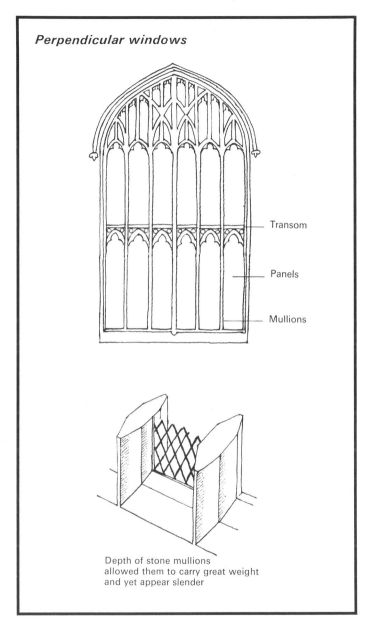

Transom

Panels

Mullions

Depth of stone mullions
allowed them to carry great weight
and yet appear slender

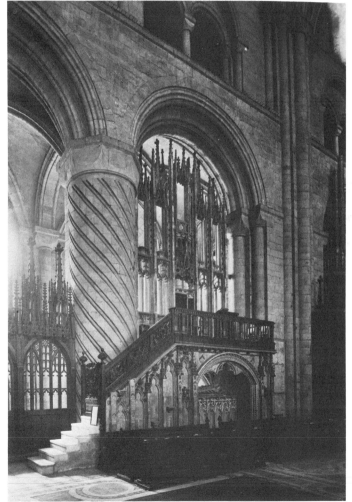

impression of weight disappeared. The mullions which ran from top to bottom of the windows helped to support the arch. But already signs of change were in the air and in less than a century a completely new style was to replace Gothic.

Durham. The bishop's throne set amongst the early Norman pillars with woodwork and stone tracery from much later in the Middle Ages.

45

English sees today

Legend:
+ Old Foundation
⊞ New Foundation (formerly monastic)
⊕ New Foundation (new see)
○ Modern Foundation

5 Cathedrals since the Middle Ages

The Reformation

During the sixteenth century, there was a revival of interest in the Roman style of architecture in southern Europe. When St Peter's in Rome, the main church in Christendom, was rebuilt in the Classical style, it was clear that the Gothic period was drawing to a close. For nearly four hundred years builders had experimented with the Gothic style, and there had been constant improvement; now it seemed as if they had answered all of the questions in the puzzle and were eager to start a new one.

In England, however, there was no longer money available for massive church building. Henry VII's break with the Catholic Church in 1534 had brought the Protestant Reformation to England and, with it, a change in attitude towards the church. The most immediate effects on the English cathedrals were that they were stripped of most of their wealth, and the ones which had been run by monks were handed over to canons. A few great churches were raised to the status of cathedrals, and they and the old monastic cathedrals became known as the cathedrals of the New Foundation.

2nd century Roman hall   627 Wooden oratory   7th century Stone church   c.780 Larger church   1100 Norman Minster

Sir Christopher Wren's great St Paul's Cathedral was built between 1675 and 1710 in the new fashion of the Renaissance, borrowed from Italian ideas.

For over a century after the Reformation the cathedrals suffered deliberate damage to many of their furnishings, especially during the period between 1649 and 1658, when England was ruled by the Puritan leader Cromwell. The Puritans believed that men might be distracted by ornate surroundings and so forget that God was more interested in the way that they thought and behaved. They feared that figure carvings and pictures, like idols, could result in ungodly superstition, and so these were ruthlessly smashed.

During the seventeenth century Christopher Wren rebuilt St Paul's after Old St Paul's had been ruined in the Great Fire.

This time chart sums up the changing history and many rebuildings of one cathedral, York. We can do little more than guess at how the earlier buildings that stood on the site looked. From Norman times we can show how the ground plan was changed, first one part of the cathedral being enlarged and then another. The thin line shows the final extent of the building, which it reached about 1500.

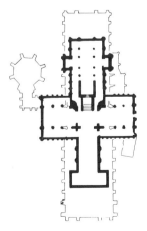

1250 New choir and Early English transepts

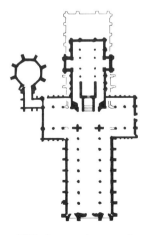

1350 Decorated nave and chapter house

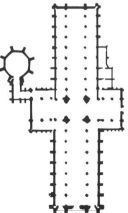

1500 Perpendicular choir

c 1970 Extensive repairs

During the eighteenth century the cathedrals were largely neglected since the Gothic style was considered barbaric and the Church was short of money.

The nineteenth century

A new interest in the Gothic style arose in the nineteenth century and this resulted in many restoration schemes. Many cathedrals were saved from serious decay, but often the work was done by people who did not understand the intentions of the medieval builders, and much of interest and value was destroyed.

Since the early nineteenth century the population of England has increased rapidly and new sees have had to be established; their cathedrals are described as Modern Foundation. This does not mean that the buildings are new; most of them were medieval monasteries or parish churches and they have simply been altered to adapt them to their new role.

During the present century three completely new buildings have gone up at Liverpool, Guildford and Coventry. The three buildings show an interesting development in twentieth-century thinking about cathedrals: Liverpool Anglican Cathedral, the earliest, is in a massive Gothic style; Guildford is in a simplified modern red-brick Gothic with light coloured stone inside; Coventry, the most recent work, is in a quite new style which owes little to the methods of earlier times.

We seem to have come to accept that each age has its own contribution to make to architecture as new material and methods are discovered. Medieval architecture is better

understood than at any time since the Middle Ages but most modern architects would wish to design in the best modern style; this, after all, is what the medieval master masons did. Building in the Gothic style would be very expensive and we expect our architects to inspire us with new creations rather than copies of the old: the new Roman Catholic Cathedral in Liverpool, the latest to be built in England, illustrates this point well.

Index

Acknowledgments

The author and publisher wish to thank the following for permission to reproduce the following illustrations:

William Shepherd, back cover; Jarrold & Sons Ltd, p. 3; National Monuments Record, pp. 4 (right), 7, 11 (left), 15 (below), 16, 24 (right), 27, 32, 33 (left), 34, 35, 36, 38, 40, 42 (right), 43, 45, 48 (left); Aerofilms Ltd, p. 5 (below); Committee for Aerial Photography, University of Cambridge, p. 5 (right); A. F. Kersting, pp. 11 (right), 44, 47, 48 (bottom); Dean and Chapter of Durham, p. 14; Walter Scott, p. 15 (above); British Library Board, pp. 17, 19, 24 (left), 30; Peter Foster and the Dean and Chapter of Lincoln, pp. 21, 29, 31; Royal Commission on Historical Monuments, Crown copyright, p. 23 (left); Trinity College, Dublin, p. 23 (right); British Travel Association, p. 33 (right); Mansell Collection, p. 41; Courtauld Institute of Art, p. 42 (left); Stewart Bale Ltd, p. 48 (top right).

Illustrations by David Harris
Maps and diagrams by Leslie Marshall
and Oxford Illustrators Ltd

front cover: *A modern artist's version of the thirteenth-century drawing shown on page 17.*

back cover: *Looking up into the lantern tower of Ely cathedral (see page 42). From the ground it appears to be made of stone, like the vaulting at York.*

The Cambridge History Library

The Cambridge Introduction to History
Written by Trevor Cairns

The Cambridge Topic Books
General Editor Trevor Cairns

The Cambridge History Library will be expanded in the future to include additional volumes. Lerner Publications Company is pleased to participate in making this excellent series of books available to a wide audience of readers.

Lerner Publications Company
241 First Avenue North, Minneapolis, Minnesota 55401